North American Trade and Travel Trends

**Bureau of
Transportation
Statistics**

U.S. Department of Transportation

Bureau of Transportation Statistics

Our mission is to lead in developing transportation data and information of high quality and to advance their effective use in both public and private transportation decisionmaking.

Our vision for the future: Data and information of high quality will support every significant transportation policy decision, thus advancing the quality of life and the economic well-being of all Americans.

To obtain North American Trade and Travel Trends and other BTS publications

Phone: 202-366-DATA [press 1]
Fax: 202-366-3197
Internet: www.bts.gov
Mail: Product Orders
            Bureau of Transportation Statistics
            U.S. Department of Transportation
            400 Seventh Street, SW, Room 3430
            Washington, DC 20590

Information Service

Email: answers@bts.gov
Phone: 800-853-1351

Recommended citation

U.S. Department of Transportation
Bureau of Transportation Statistics
North American Trade and Travel Trends, BTS01-07
Washington, DC: 2001

Acknowledgments

U.S. Department of Transportation

Norman Y. Mineta
Secretary

Michael P. Jackson
Deputy Secretary

Bureau of Transportation Statistics

Ashish K. Sen
Director

Rick Kowalewski
Deputy Director

Susan J. Lapham
Associate Director for Statistical Programs

John V. Wells
Chief Economist

Produced under the direction of:

Wendell Fletcher
Assistant Director for Transportation Analysis

Project Manager

Lisa Randall

Editor

Marsha Fenn

Major Contributors

Felix Ammah-Tagoe
William Mallett
Marcus Mathias

Other Contributors

Elijah Henley
John Bushery
Martha Courtney
Dorinda Edmondson
Steve Lewis
Matthew Sheppard
Lorisa Smith

Cover Design

Colabours
Communications Inc.

Table of Contents

List of Tables

List of Figures

Maps

Boxes

North American Trade and Travel Trends

Canada and Mexico are the United States' largest trading and travel partners—accounting for one-third of the value of U.S. international trade—and are the top destinations for Americans traveling abroad. Since the North American Free Trade Agreement (NAFTA) came into effect in January 1994, Canada's and Mexico's shares of overall U.S. international trade and travel have grown.

This cross-border trade and travel represents a large amount of economic activity, commerce, and tourism of benefit to all three countries. In 2000, the value of U.S. merchandise trade with Canada and Mexico was $653 billion. Canadians and Mexicans spent nearly $15 billion for travel or fares to visit the United States. U.S. travelers spent approximately the same amount in Canada and Mexico.

As trade and travel increase, questions about how they affect the U.S. transportation system have become prominent (e.g., are facilities at land border crossings, seaports, airports, and intermodal terminals and connectors able to meet passenger and freight demand?). Like other transportation demands, increased trade and travel can affect competition for network space, scheduling, capacity needs, congestion, safety and security, and the environment. Increases in trucks and personal-use vehicles crossing the borders and changes in modal shares could result in bottlenecks at the dominant border crossing points and operational inefficiencies in the movement of people and freight. In addition, heightened security requirements will also affect the flow of goods and people across U.S. borders.

This report examines recent trends in U.S. international trade and passenger travel with Canada and Mexico.[1] It also reviews modal shares of NAFTA-partner trade and travel, examines the geography of the trade and travel flows, and identifies key influencing factors. Table 1 provides summary data on trade and

---

[1] Except where noted, this report generally examines *trade* trends for the 1994 to 2000 time period. *Overnight travel* is examined through 2000. However, due to limitations of data availability, *same-day travel* and *overall travel* trends are generally reviewed through 1999.

Table 1
Trends in U.S. International Trade, Trade with Canada and Mexico, Population, GDP, and Passenger Trips

	1990	1995	2000	Percentage change, 1990–2000	Annual growth rate (percent)
Population (millions)					
United States	249	263	281	13.2	1.2
Canada	28	30	31	10.6	1.0
Mexico	81	91	97	19.9	1.8
Gross domestic product (GDP)					
United States (billions of current $US)	5,744	7,270	9,963	73.5	5.7
United States (billions of chained 1996 $US)[1]	6,708	7,544	9,319	38.9	3.3
Canada (billions of current $US)	540	546	699	29.5	2.6
Mexico (billions of current $US)	240	262	575	139.0	9.1
Value of total U.S. international merchandise trade					
Billions of current dollars	907	1,341	1,997	120.3	8.2
Billions of chained 1996 dollars[1]	891	1,308	2,163	142.7	9.3
Value of U.S. trade with NAFTA partners (billions of current $US)	233	380	653	179.9	10.8
Thousands of passenger trips between the United States and:					
Canada	105,167	89,484	86,827[2]	–17.4[2]	–2.1
Mexico	178,949	185,628	212,321[2]	18.6[2]	1.9

[1] To compare economic changes over time, current or nominal values of currencies must be deflated or adjusted for inflation. In the United States, the Bureau of Economic Analysis (BEA) establishes indices to calculate changes between years. These are used to calculate real chained dollars. Annual changes in the indices are chained (multiplied) together to form a time series. Chained dollars, instead of merely reflecting inflation, capture the effect of relative changes in prices and in the composition of output. They also better reflect cyclical fluctuations in the economy. Chained 1996 dollars are the most currently available indices from BEA for adjusting for inflation.

[2] For this category, the last data year is 1999, not 2000, and the percentage change column covers 1990–1999.

SOURCES: **Data for trade, population, and GDP for 1990 and 1995**—U.S. Department of Transportation, Bureau of Transportation Statistics; U.S. Department of Commerce, U.S. Census Bureau; Statistics Canada; Transport Canada; Instituto Mexicano del Transporte; Instituto Nacional de Estadística, Geografía e Informática; and Secretaría de Comunicaciones y Transportes, *North American Transportation in Figures: English Edition*, BTS00-05 (Washington, DC: Bureau of Transportation Statistics, 2000).

Trade data for 2000—Based on U.S. Department of Commerce, U.S. Census Bureau, U.S. Merchandise Trade Data; and U.S. Department of Transportation, Bureau of Transportation Statistics, Transborder Surface Freight Data.

U.S. population data for 2000—U.S. Department of Commerce, U.S. Census Bureau.

Canadian population data for 2000—Statistics Canada.

Mexican population data for 2000—Instituto Nacional de Estadística, Geografía e Informática, available at http://www.inegi.gob.mx/estadistica/ingles/sociodem/fisociodemografia.html.

U.S. GDP for 2000—U.S. Department of Commerce, Bureau of Economic Analysis data, available at http://www.ita.doc.gov/td/industry/otea/usfth/aggregate/HL00T05.txt.

Canadian GDP for 2000—Statistics Canada, available at http://www.statcan.ca/english/Pgdb/Economy/econom.htm#nat.

Mexican GDP for 2000—Instituto Nacional de Estadística, Geografía e Informática, available at http://www.inegi.gob.mx/estadistica/ingles/economia/fieconomia.html.

Data for passenger trips between the United States and Canada—Statistics Canada, *International Travel, Travel Between Canada and Other Countries (Touriscope)*, Catalogue No. 66-201-XPB (Ottawa, Ontario: Various years).

Data for passenger trips between the United States and Mexico—Banco de México, Dirección General de Investigación Económica, Dirección de Medición Económica, Mexico City, D.F., 1999 and 2001.

travel and context information about the population and economy of the three countries.

U.S. Trade with Canada and Mexico

From 1990 to 2000, the value of U.S. international trade worldwide more than doubled in inflation-adjusted terms, rising from $891 billion to $2.2 trillion. In 2000, nearly one-third of U.S. merchandise trade was with Canada and Mexico, a slight increase from 29 percent in 1994 (table 2). Most of this rise can be attributed to U.S. trade with Mexico, which grew from 8.5 percent to 12.4 percent of total U.S. international merchandise trade during this period. Trade with Canada remained, on average, about one-fifth of total U.S. trade.

Between 1994 and 2000, the value of U.S. merchandise trade with Canada and Mexico grew at an average annual rate of 11 percent,[2] while growth in U.S. trade with the rest of the world averaged 8 percent per year[3] (table 2). U.S. trade with Canada, our number one trading partner for decades, increased (in current U.S. dollars) from $243 billion to $406 billion in 2000, an average annual rate of 8.9 percent.[4] Trade with Mexico grew by 16 percent per year, from about $100 billion in 1994 to $248 billion in 2000. (Mexico became our second largest trading partner, surpassing Japan in 1999.) The growth in trade with Mexico occurred despite the decline in exports to Mexico in 1995 due to the peso crisis and the related economic recession. U.S. exports to Mexico recovered quickly after the Mexican economy began to stabilize and grow[5] (figure 1).

Between 1994 and 2000, the U.S. merchandise trade deficit with NAFTA partners increased from $13 billion to $77

[2] In comparison to the 11 percent annual growth rate between 1994 and 2000 in current dollars, in inflation-adjusted terms, U.S.-NAFTA-partner merchandise trade averaged 12 percent per year in real (chained 1996) dollars. Although growth rates for the entire economy that have been adjusted for inflation are often lower than those based on current dollars, this is not always the case if a country's merchandise trade is growing faster than gross domestic product (GDP). Therefore, U.S.-NAFTA trade grew at a slightly faster rate in real (chained dollar) terms, in part because of the lower inflation rate in the United States and the growth of U.S. GDP.

[3] Compared with 9 percent in inflation-adjusted real (chained 1996) dollars.

[4] Detailed indices are unavailable to deflate the trade data for imports and exports at the country level and for mode of transportation and commodity groupings. Adjusting for inflation is important to reflect the correct size of the change in the value of trade. Without adjusting for inflation, it is difficult to determine how changes in the value of merchandise affect the volume of goods transported.

[5] Pre-peso-crisis levels of exports were reached within 17 months, compared with the 7 years it took to regain export levels following Mexico's 1982 economic crisis.

Table 2
**Value of U.S. Merchandise Trade with Canada and Mexico Compared with
U.S. Trade with All Other Countries: 1994–2000**

	Total U.S. international trade (current $ millions)	U.S. trade with NAFTA partners (current $ millions)	U.S. trade with all other countries (current $ millions)	Ratio of U.S.-NAFTA to all U.S. trade (percent)
1994	1,175,883	342,923	832,960	29.2
1995	1,328,285	379,989	948,296	28.6
1996	1,420,364	421,192	999,172	29.7
1997	1,557,472	475,382	1,082,090	30.5
1998	1,594,000	502,715	1,091,285	31.5
1999	1,717,587	558,987	1,158,600	32.5
2000	1,997,306	653,270	1,344,036	32.7
Percentage change, 1994 –2000	69.9	90.5	61.4	
Annual growth rate, 1994 –2000 (percent)	9.2	11.3	8.3	

SOURCES: U.S. Department of Transportation, Bureau of Transportation Statistics, special tabulation, April 2001; based on: **total trade, air and water**—U.S. Department of Commerce, U.S. Census Bureau, Foreign Trade Division, *FT920 U.S. Merchandise Trade* (Washington, DC: Various years); **all land modes**—U.S. Department of Transportation, Bureau of Transportation Statistics, Transborder Surface Freight Data.

Figure 1
Value of U.S. Merchandise Trade with Canada and Mexico: 1994–2000

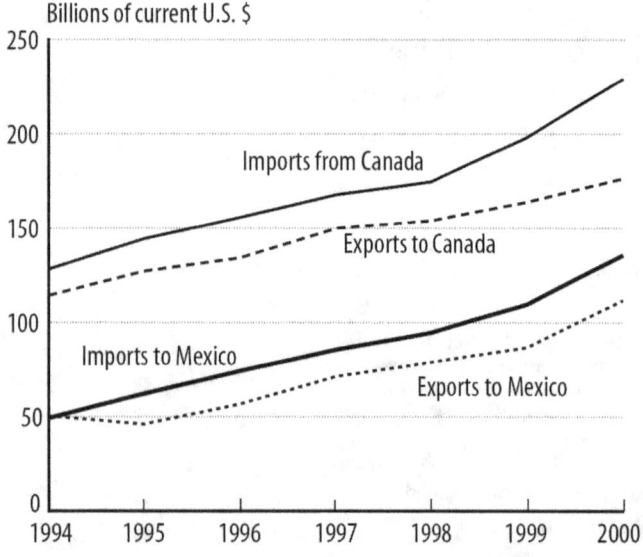

SOURCES: U.S. Department of Transportation, Bureau of Transportation Statistics, special tabulation, April 2001; based on: **total trade, air and water**—U.S. Department of Commerce, U.S. Census Bureau, Foreign Trade Division, *FT920 U.S. Merchandise Trade* (Washington, DC: Various years); **all land modes**—U.S. Department of Transportation, Bureau of Transportation Statistics, Transborder Surface Freight Data.

billion in current dollars (figure 2). The sustained growth of the U.S. economy, shifting exchange rates, and the exceptional market opportunities here spurred the flow of imports and increased the U.S. trade deficit. During this period, NAFTA-partner imports into the United States rose at an average annual rate of 12.7 percent compared with 9.7 percent for exports. U.S. imports from Canada grew by 10 percent annually and imports from Mexico rose by 18 percent. Exports to Canada grew by 7.5 percent while exports to Mexico grew by 14.1 percent annually. Since 1998, the U.S. trade deficit with Canada has increased at a faster rate than that with Mexico.

Modal Shares of NAFTA Trade

Modal shares of NAFTA trade differ depending on whether the value of the trade or its weight is examined (box 1). In terms of value, trucks transported about two-thirds of the goods in U.S.-NAFTA-partner trade in 2000 (figure 3). Trucks carried $429 billion ($212 billion of exports and $217 billion of imports) of NAFTA-partner trade, up from $323 billion in 1997 (in current U.S. dollars). Trucking was followed by rail, air, water, and pipeline. Between 1997 and 2000, trucks transported about 75 percent of the U.S.-NAFTA-partner exports and about 63 percent of the imports by value. Trucks were more dominant in U.S. trade with Mexico, averaging about 72 percent, than in U.S. trade with Canada, averaging about 66 percent. Between 1997 and 2000, while the share of

Figure 2
Balance of U.S. Merchandise Trade with Canada and Mexico: 1994–2000

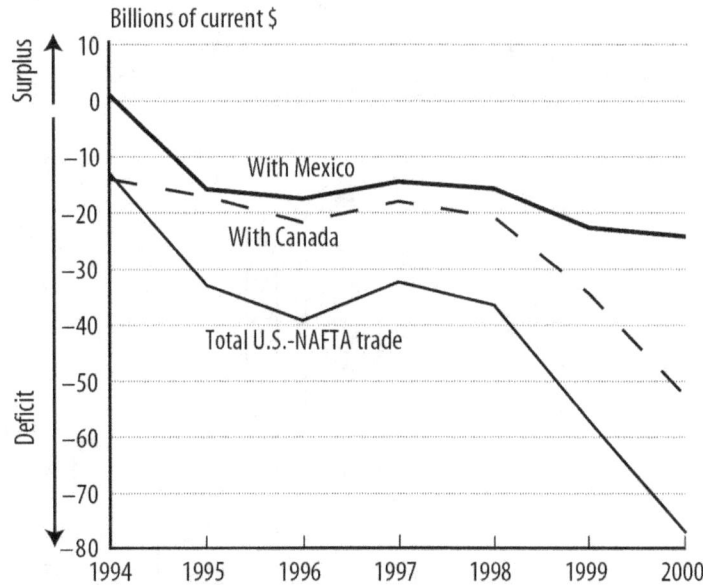

SOURCES: U.S. Department of Transportation, Bureau of Transportation Statistics, special tabulation, April 2001; based on: **total trade, air and water**—U.S. Department of Commerce, U.S. Census Bureau, Foreign Trade Division, *FT920 U.S. Merchandise Trade* (Washington, DC: Various years); **all land modes**—U.S. Department of Transportation, Bureau of Transportation Statistics, Transborder Surface Freight Data.

Box 1
International Merchandise Trade Data Sources

This report uses trade data from many sources: the Census Bureau's U.S. Merchandise Trade data, the Bureau of Economic Analysis' (BEA) balance of payments trade data, the Bureau of Transportation Statistics' (BTS) Transborder Surface Freight Data, and the U.S. Customs Service's border-crossing data.

Data on U.S. total international merchandise trade and trade by air and water modes are from the Census Bureau's Foreign Trade Division. U.S. total merchandise trade data in inflation-adjusted terms are from BEA. These inflation-adjusted data, however, are not available for imports and exports at the country level and for mode of transportation and type of commodities. Consequently, this report uses current dollar data for most of the trade discussions. Data on merchandise trade transported by all land modes, including data on commodity groups, and origins and destinations of the trade flows, are from the BTS Transborder Surface Freight Data.

The report also uses U.S. Customs Service data on trucks crossing into the United States from Canada and Mexico. These data represent the number of truck crossings into the United States, including both loaded and unloaded trucks. The data do not count individual unique vehicles. For example, one truck may cross the border multiple times in one day. Each crossing would be counted. The data also do not provide information on the goods carried by the trucks or the U.S. destinations.

Traded goods usually move by more than one mode of transportation from origin to final destination. In U.S. trade statistics, the export mode of transportation is the mode used when the U.S. international border is crossed. For imports, the mode of transportation is the last mode used when the freight was transported to the U.S. port of clearance or entry. The available trade data do not distinguish goods moved by intermodal combinations.

Figure 3
**Modal Shares of U.S. Merchandise Trade with NAFTA
Partners by Value: 1997–2000**

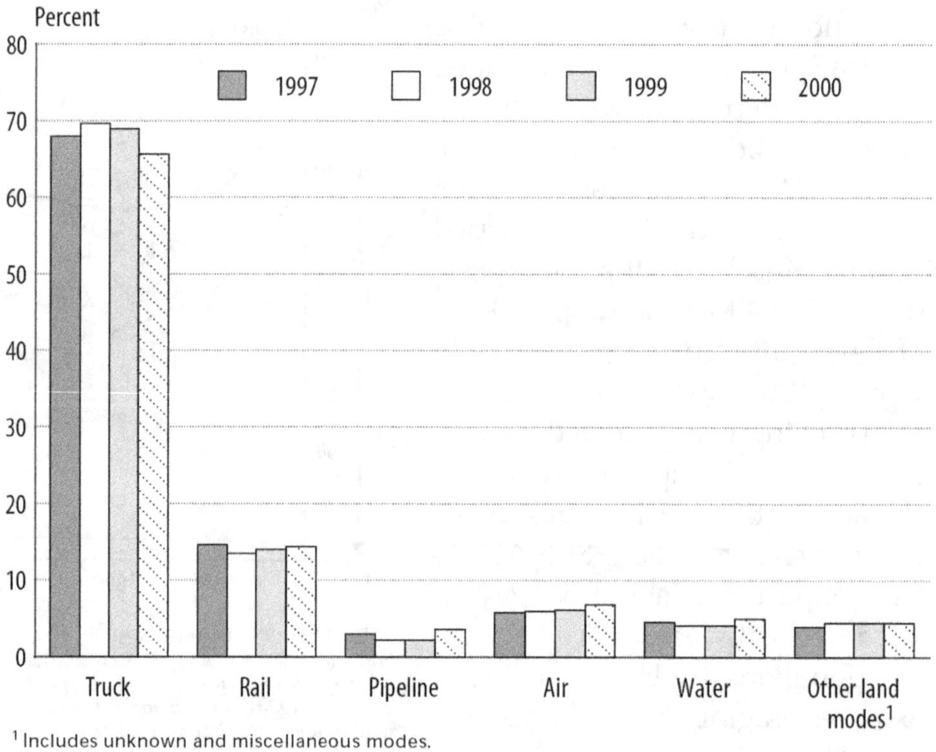

Percent

¹ Includes unknown and miscellaneous modes.

SOURCES: U.S. Department of Transportation, Bureau of Transportation Statistics, special tabulation, April 2001; based on: **total trade, air and wate**r—U.S. Department of Commerce, U.S. Census Bureau, Foreign Trade Division, *FT920 U.S. Merchandise Trade* (Washington, DC: Various years); **all land modes**—U.S. Department of Transportation, Bureau of Transportation Statistics, Transborder Surface Freight Data.

NAFTA-partner trade transported by truck and rail remained fairly stable, air transportation and pipeline increased the fastest and their shares of the value of trade rose slightly (table 3).

A different picture of modal shares emerges when U.S. NAFTA-partner trade is measured by the weight[6] of the traded goods (figure 4). In 2000, trucks moved an estimated 190 million tons of traded goods with Canada and Mexico, accounting for about 35 percent of the weight of U.S.-NAFTA-partner trade. An estimated 175 million tons traveled over water, accounting for just under one-third of the weight. Water transportation was followed by rail, pipeline, and air. Modal shares by weight vary by imports and exports. In 2000, trucks transported 26 percent of import tonnage compared with an estimated 56 percent of exports (table 4).

[6] Total weight data are Bureau of Transportation Statistics (BTS) estimates, based on U.S. Census Bureau tonnage data for imports into the United States and BTS estimates of tonnage for U.S. exports using value-to-weight ratios from the import data.

Table 3
Value of U.S. Merchandise Trade with NAFTA Partners by Mode: 1997–2000
(Millions of dollars)

Mode	1997	1998	1999	2000	Percentage change, 1997–2000
Truck	323,298	349,979	385,413	428,700	32.6
Rail	69,844	67,872	78,414	94,198	34.9
Air	27,744	30,127	34,380	44,950	62.0
Water	21,661	20,852	23,357	32,607	50.5
Pipeline	14,132	11,289	12,315	23,592	66.9
Other[1]	18,704	22,596	25,107	29,224	56.2
Total trade	**475,382**	**502,715**	**558,987**	**653,270**	**37.4**
Subtotal, land	425,977	451,736	501,239	575,713	35.2
Land, % of total	89.6	89.9	89.7	88.1	

[1] Other includes "flyaway aircraft" (i.e., aircraft moving under its own power from the manufacturer to a customer and not carrying freight), vessels moving under their own power, pedestrians carrying freight, and miscellaneous.

NOTES: Shipments that neither originate nor terminate in the United States (i.e., in-transit or in-bond shipments) are not included here, although they use the U.S. transportation system. These shipments are usually part of Mexico-Canada trade, and simply pass through the United States. Merchandise trade data exclude export shipments valued at less than $2,500 and import shipments valued at less than $1,250. Individual modal totals may not sum to exact export or import totals due to rounding.

SOURCES: U.S. Department of Transportation, Bureau of Transportation Statistics, special tabulation, April 2001; based on: **total trade, air and water**—U.S. Department of Commerce, U.S. Census Bureau, Foreign Trade Division, *FT920 U.S. Merchandise Trade* (Washington, DC: Various years); **all land modes**— U.S. Department of Transportation, Bureau of Transportation Statistics, Transborder Surface Freight Data.

Modal shares by weight also vary for U.S.-Canada and U.S.-Mexico trade. For U.S. trade with Canada, trucks moved 41 percent of the tonnage, followed by rail (24 percent), pipeline (22 percent), water (13 percent), and air (0.2 percent). For U.S. trade with Mexico, water transportation dominated with 69 percent of the weight, followed by trucks (24 percent), rail (6 percent), pipeline (2 percent), and air (0.1 percent).[7] It is possible that under full liberalization of access for trucking in the United States and Mexico, the truck share of import tonnage could increase.[8]

---

[7] The high modal share for U.S. waterborne trade with Mexico is primarily attributed to the Gulf of Mexico trade in petroleum products and other bulk commodities.

[8] NAFTA set a timetable for truck carrier access to the United States by Mexican carriers. The agreement called for access to Mexican border states for U.S. and Canadian carriers and for Mexican carrier access to U.S. border states to begin in December 1995. Under the treaty, all access limits on commercial trucking between the United States and Mexico were to be phased out by January 1, 2000. Currently, however, Mexican trucks have access only to designated commercial zones extending 20 miles from U.S. border cities. Canadian trucks can travel anywhere in the United States provided they comply with U.S. regulations; however, Canadian firms cannot provide point-to-point service within the United States.

Figure 4
Modal Shares of U.S. NAFTA-Partner Merchandise Trade by Value and Weight: 2000

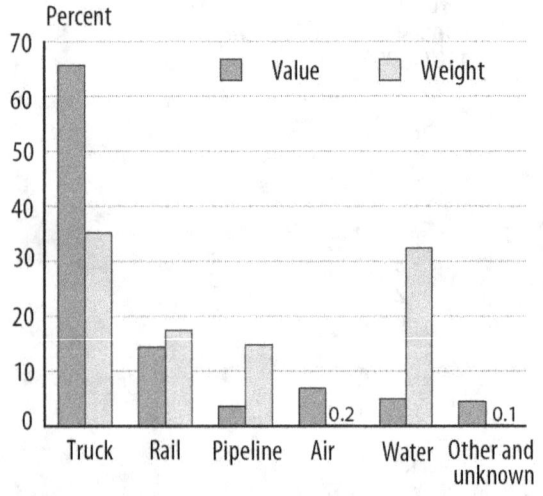

SOURCES: U.S. Department of Transportation, Bureau of Transportation Statistics, special tabulation, April 2001; based on: **total trade, air and water**—U.S. Department of Commerce, U.S. Census Bureau, Foreign Trade Division, *FT920 U.S. Merchandise Trade* (Washington, DC: Various years); **all land modes**—U.S. Department of Transportation, Bureau of Transportation Statistics, Transborder Surface Freight Data.

Table 4
U.S. Merchandise Trade with Canada and Mexico by Mode: 2000

Mode	Value (percent)	Weight (percent)
NAFTA trade, total	**100.0**	**100.0**
Truck	65.6	35.1
Rail	14.4	17.4
Pipeline	3.6	14.8
Air	6.9	0.2
Water	5.0	32.4
Other and unknown	4.5	0.1
U.S.-NAFTA imports, total	**100.0**	**100.0**
Truck	59.3	25.7
Rail	19.4	19.8
Pipeline	6.3	20.5
Air	4.9	0.1
Water	6.4	33.9
Other and unknown	3.7	0.1
U.S.-NAFTA exports, total	**100.0**	**100.0**
Truck	73.6	55.7
Rail	8.1	12.3
Pipeline	0.2	2.3
Air	9.3	0.4
Water	3.2	29.2
Other and unknown	5.5	0.2

SOURCES: U.S. Department of Transportation, Bureau of Transportation Statistics, June 2001; based on: **total, water and air data**—U.S. Department of Commerce, U.S. Census Bureau, Foreign Trade Division, *U.S. Exports of Merchandise CD* and *U.S. Imports of Merchandise CD*, December 2000; **truck, rail, pipeline, other and unknown data**—U.S. Department of Transportation, Bureau of Transportation Statistics, Transborder Surface Freight Data, 2000; and special tabulations.

Geography of North American Trade

Many factors affect the magnitude and distribution of NAFTA trade among U.S. states, including proximity to the Canadian and Mexican borders, location of dominant border ports, size of the state's population and economy, and its manufacturing base. Not surprisingly, 9 of the top 10 origins and destinations by value are border states with large manufacturing bases, such as Michigan, Texas, California, New York, and Ohio (figure 5).

Figure 5
Top 25 States Engaging in NAFTA Land Trade by Value: 1995 and 2000

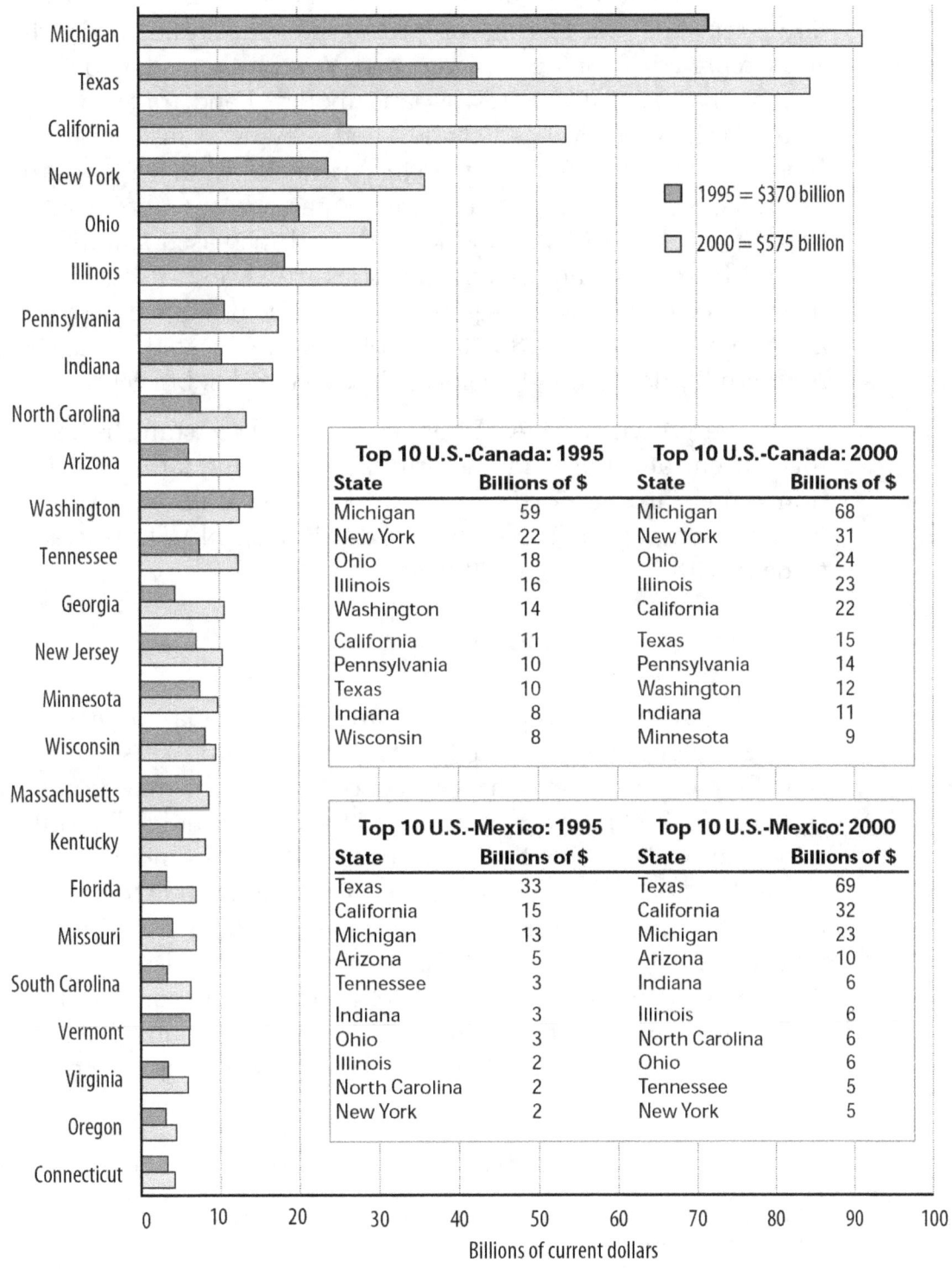

Legend:
■ 1995 = $370 billion
□ 2000 = $575 billion

Top 10 U.S.-Canada: 1995		Top 10 U.S.-Canada: 2000	
State	Billions of $	State	Billions of $
Michigan	59	Michigan	68
New York	22	New York	31
Ohio	18	Ohio	24
Illinois	16	Illinois	23
Washington	14	California	22
California	11	Texas	15
Pennsylvania	10	Pennsylvania	14
Texas	10	Washington	12
Indiana	8	Indiana	11
Wisconsin	8	Minnesota	9

Top 10 U.S.-Mexico: 1995		Top 10 U.S.-Mexico: 2000	
State	Billions of $	State	Billions of $
Texas	33	Texas	69
California	15	California	32
Michigan	13	Michigan	23
Arizona	5	Arizona	10
Tennessee	3	Indiana	6
Indiana	3	Illinois	6
Ohio	3	North Carolina	6
Illinois	2	Ohio	6
North Carolina	2	Tennessee	5
New York	2	New York	5

Billions of current dollars

NOTE: Land trade includes truck, rail, pipeline, and miscellaneous and unknown modes.

SOURCES: U.S. Department of Transportation, Bureau of Transportation Statistics, Transborder Surface Freight Data, 1995 and 2000.

U.S.-NAFTA-partner land trade[9] is highly concentrated among the U.S. states, with the 10 largest states accounting for about 67 percent of the value of total land trade in 2000, up from 64 percent in 1995. During this period, North Carolina and Arizona replaced Washington State and Wisconsin in the top 10 NAFTA-partner trade states by land modes. Land trade to and from Washington declined slightly and grew at a faster rate in North Carolina and Arizona than in Wisconsin. Trade with North Carolina, a nonborder state, rose in part because of in-state growth in automobile manufacturing and increased shipments to and from the maquiladora factories[10] in Mexico. By 2000, there were about 3,600 maquiladora manufacturing plants operating in Mexico. About 80 percent of these are located in the six northern border states of Mexico, close to the U.S. border.[11]

The growth of NAFTA land trade in U.S. states reflects the concentration of manufacturing activities and large population centers in the northeast, midwest, California, and Texas (see map on page 11). Nearly one-third of all NAFTA surface trade is with Michigan, California, and Texas.

Land Ports and Border Crossings

There are over 75 land ports along the U.S.-Canada border and over 25 along the U.S-Mexico border.[12] Nevertheless, U.S.-NAFTA-partner trade is heavily concentrated at a few border crossings. In 2000, 10 ports accounted for 73 percent of all North American trade by land, with Detroit, Michigan, and Laredo, Texas, handling the majority of land trade on each U.S. border (figure 6). Border crossings at Detroit handled $94 billion worth of NAFTA trade in 2000, accounting for 16 percent of the U.S. land trade, down from 22 percent in 1995. Laredo's share increased from 8 percent to 15 percent, handling $84 billion worth of NAFTA trade in 2000. Among the top 20 ports,

---

[9] Land or surface trade refers to trade by truck, rail, pipeline, and miscellaneous and unknown modes.

[10] Maquiladoras are manufacturing plants concentrated on the northern Mexican border that make goods from imported components for re-export to the United States.

[11] J.P. McCray and R. Harrison, *North American Free Trade Agreement Trucks on U.S. Highway Corridors*, Transportation Research Record 1653 (Washington, DC: National Academy Press, 1999), pp. 79–85.

[12] These are U.S. Customs ports that may include more than one crossing point. For example, there are four bridge crossings at the Customs port of Laredo, TX.

Change in Value of U.S.-NAFTA-Partner Land Trade by State: 1995–2000

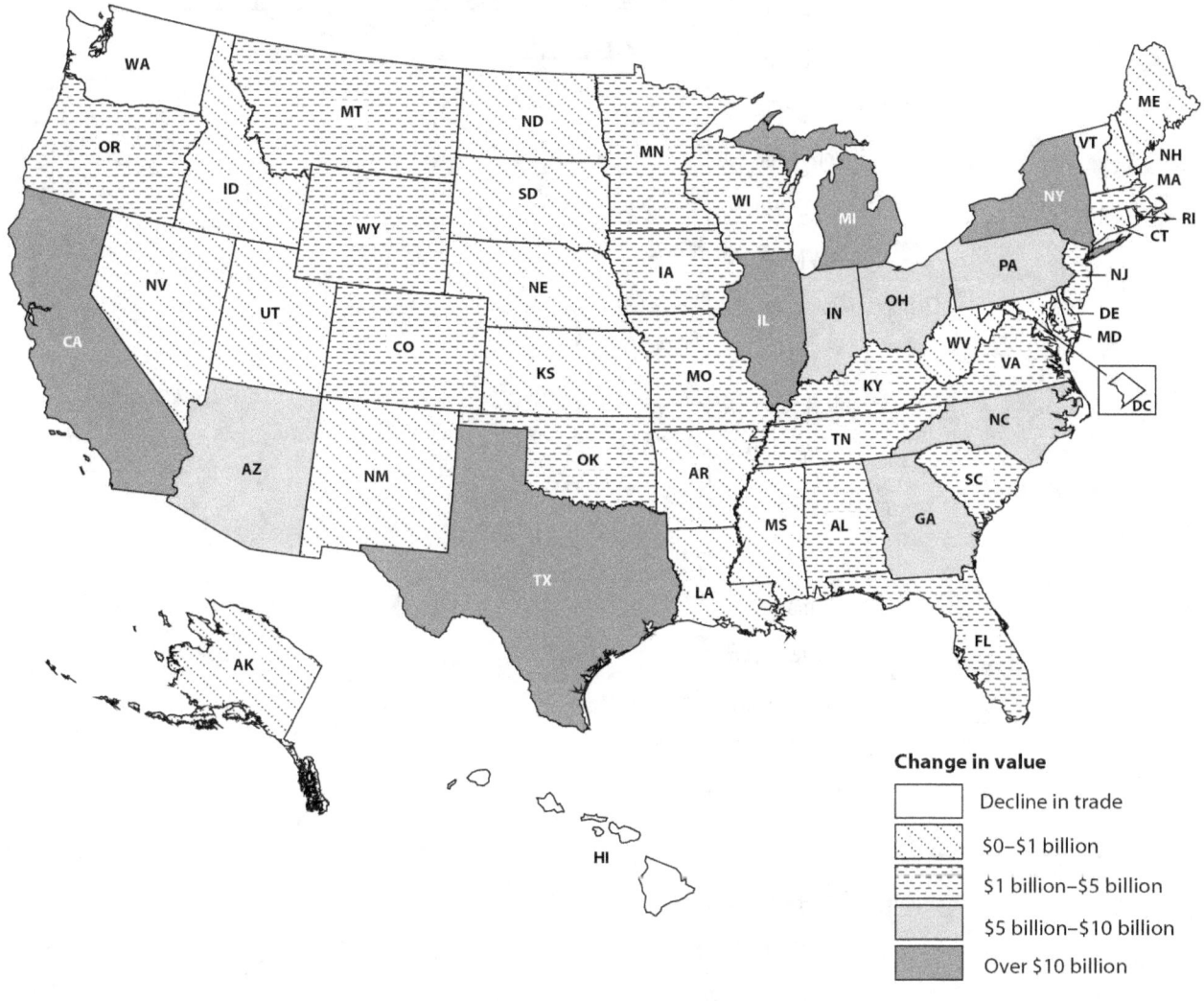

Change in value

	Decline in trade
	$0–$1 billion
	$1 billion–$5 billion
	$5 billion–$10 billion
	Over $10 billion

NOTE: Land trade includes truck, rail, pipeline, and miscellaneous and unknown modes.

SOURCES: U.S. Department of Transportation, Bureau of Transportation Statistics, Transborder Surface Freight Data, 1995 and 2000.

trade passing through Laredo, Texas, grew the fastest and trade passing through Highgate Springs, Vermont, declined slightly.

The concentration of origins and destinations of U.S.-NAFTA-partner land trade in large population and manufacturing centers and the flow of trade through dominant ports of entry have major impacts on the U.S. transportation network, particularly on major border entry points and north-south highway corridors. In 2000, there were over 11.5 million commercial truck

Figure 6
Top 20 NAFTA Land Ports: 1995 and 2000
(Percentage of value)

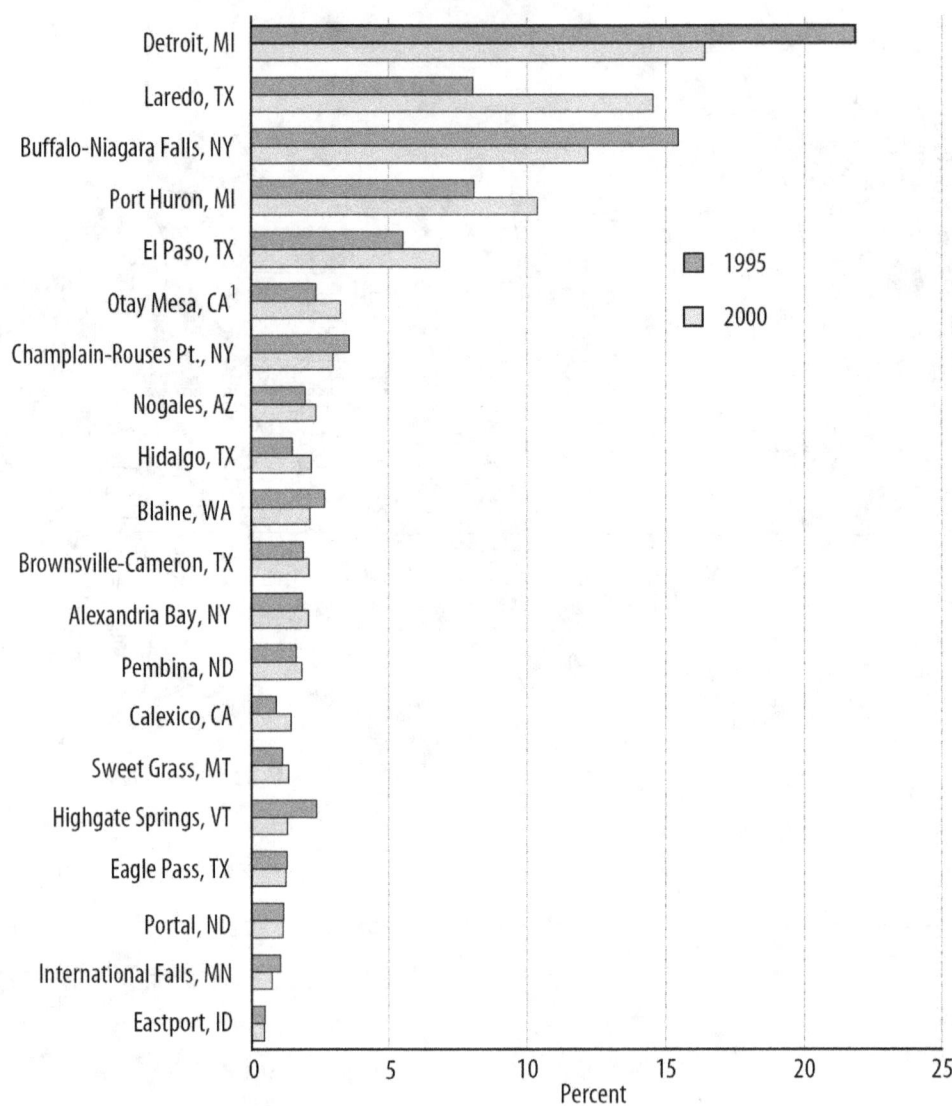

¹ 1995 data for Otay Mesa, CA, include traffic
crossing the border at San Ysidro, CA, which has
since been closed to truck traffic.

NOTE: Land trade includes truck, rail, pipeline,
and miscellaneous and unknown modes.

SOURCES: U.S. Department of Transportation,
Bureau of Transportation Statistics, Transborder
Surface Freight Data, 1995 and 2000.

crossings[13] into the United States from Canada and Mexico, up
26 percent from 9 million in 1997 (table 5). Commercial trucks
entering the United States at the busiest crossing points—Detroit,

[13] This number is crossings, not the number of unique individual vehicles and includes both
loaded and unloaded trucks. For example, one truck may cross the border multiple times in one
day. Each crossing would be counted. For U.S.-Mexico trade, Mexican commercial carriers currently enter the 20-mile border zone where the cargo is offloaded into warehouses or onto other
carriers' vehicles (e.g., trucks or trains) for transport to the final U.S. destination.

Table 5
Top 20 NAFTA Border Truck Crossings into the United States: 1997 and 2000

Rank in 2000	Port name	1997 (thousands)	2000 (thousands)	Average number of truck crossings per day (2000)	1997 (percent)	2000 (percent)	Percentage change, 1997–2000
1	Detroit, MI	1,420	1,769	4,848	15.4	15.3	24.6
2	Laredo, TX	1,251	1,493	4,091	13.6	12.9	19.3
3	Buffalo-Niagara, NY	1,054	1,198	3,282	11.4	10.4	13.7
4	Port Huron, MI	679	839	2,299	7.4	7.3	23.5
5	El Paso, TX	583	720	1,974	6.3	6.2	23.6
6	Otay Mesa/San Ysidro, CA	568	688	1,886	6.2	5.9	21.2
7	Blaine, WA	463	517	1,416	5.0	4.5	11.6
8	Champlain-Rouses Pt., NY	299	391	1,071	3.2	3.4	30.7
9	Hidalgo, TX	235	374	1,025	2.5	3.2	59.3
10	Brownsville, TX	248	299	820	2.7	2.6	20.9
11	Calexico East/Calexico, CA	U	279	764	U	2.4	U
12	Alexandria Bay, NY	220	278	763	2.4	2.4	26.5
13	Nogales, AZ	243	255	698	2.6	2.2	4.9
14	Pembina, ND	152	214	587	1.7	1.9	40.9
15	Calais, ME	126	154	422	1.4	1.3	22.5
16	Sweetgrass, MT	112	146	400	1.2	1.3	30.5
17	Derby Line, VT	101	139	380	1.1	1.2	37.6
18	Houlton, ME	103	133	364	1.1	1.1	28.8
19	Highgate Springs, VT	99	133	364	1.1	1.1	33.9
20	Jackman, ME	87	128	350	0.9	1.1	47.1
	Total, top 20 ports	**8,041**	**10,148**	**27,802**	**87.3**	**87.7**	**26.2**
	Total, all ports	**9,215**	**11,574**	**31,709**	**100.0**	**100.0**	**25.6**

KEY: U = data are unavailable.

NOTE: Data represent the number of truck crossings, not the number of unique vehicles, and include both loaded and unloaded trucks. Data for the port of Calexico is typically reported as a combined total with Calexico East.

SOURCES: U.S. Department of Transportation, Bureau of Transportation Statistics, special tabulations, May 2001; based on data from U.S. Department of Treasury, U.S. Customs Service, Mission Support Services, Office of Field Operations.

Michigan (15 percent) and Laredo, Texas (13 percent)—create a dominant north-south truck corridor (from Detroit through Memphis, Tennessee, and San Antonio, Texas, to Laredo). Among the top 20 border crossings, truck traffic at Hidalgo, Texas, increased the fastest between 1997 and 2000, followed by Jackman, Maine, and Pembina, North Dakota.

If U.S. trade with Canada and Mexico continues at its current growth rate and keeps pace with trends in the U.S. economy, trucking's large share of NAFTA freight may well continue, creating new challenges for highway capacity and border crossing infrastructure.

Table 6
**Top 10 Commodities by Value in U.S. Merchandise Trade with NAFTA Partners
for All Land Modes: 1995 and 2000**
(Current U.S. dollars)

Rank in 2000	Commodity description	Value ($ billions)	Percent	Rank in 1995	Commodity description	Value ($ billions)	Percent
1	Motor vehicles, parts, and accessories	125	21.7	1	Motor vehicles, parts, and accessories	82	22.1
2	Electrical machinery and equipment and parts	89	15.5	2	Nuclear reactors, machinery, and mechanical appliances	48	13.1
3	Nuclear reactors, machinery, and mechanical appliances	75	13.0	3	Electrical machinery and equipment and parts	48	13.1
4	Mineral fuels, mineral oils, and products	31	5.3	4	Mineral fuels, mineral oils, and products	14	3.7
5	Plastics and related products	22	3.8	5	Special classification provisions	13	3.5
6	Special classification provisions	21	3.6	6	Paper, paperboard, and paper products	13	3.4
7	Paper, paperboard, and paper products	16	2.8	7	Plastics and related products	12	3.3
8	Wood and articles of wood; wood charcoal	13	2.3	8	Aircraft, spacecraft, and parts thereof	12	3.2
9	Furniture, furnishings, and lighting products	13	2.3	9	Wood and articles of wood; wood charcoal	9	2.4
10	Optical, photographic, and precision	13	2.3	10	Optical, photographic, and precision	8	2.1
	Total, top 10 commodities	**418**	**72.6**		**Total, top 10 commodities**	**259**	**69.9**
	Total, all commodities	**576**	**100.0**		**Total, all commodities**	**370**	**100.0**

NOTE: Land trade includes truck, rail, pipeline, and miscellaneous and unknown modes.

SOURCE: U.S. Department of Transportation, Bureau of Transportation Statistics, Transborder Surface Freight Data, 1995 and 2000.

Changes in Commodity Mix

Manufactured goods have been key to the expansion in U.S. trade with Canada and Mexico. Motor vehicles, parts, and accessories have dominated NAFTA trade by value as North American automobile manufacturing is increasingly integrated across the three countries. Table 6 shows rankings of the top 10 commodity groups by value of U.S.-NAFTA-partner land trade. In 2000, trade in motor vehicles, parts, and accessories was valued at $125 billion, accounting for 22 percent of land trade with NAFTA partners, a proportion that has remained stable since 1995. The 10 leading commodity groups in 2000 accounted for 73 percent of the land trade compared with 70 percent in 1995. Over this period, furniture and furnishing products almost doubled in value, advancing from 11th in rank to 9th, and replacing aircraft equipment and parts in the top 10 commodity groups.

Aircraft equipment and parts declined from $12 billion in 1995 to $5 billion in 2000. Exports of aircraft equipment and parts to Canada by land modes dropped from $10 billion to $1 billion while imports from Mexico dropped from $145 million to $62 million.

Among the top 10 industry groups, the fastest growing commodities transported by land modes were mineral fuels and related goods (including petroleum products), furniture and furnishing products, and electrical and electronics, which were up by 123 percent, 97 percent, and 84 percent, respectively. Overall, the fastest growing goods moving over land were textile products (knitted or crocheted fabrics) followed by apparel and clothing accessories, and cotton.

Factors of Change

Several factors account for the growth in U.S. trade with Canada and Mexico, including greater U.S. direct investment abroad (USDIA), fluctuations in exchange rates, changes in industry manufacturing and distribution patterns, and the rising gross domestic product (GDP) in all three countries. As shown in table 1 (page 2), U.S. GDP grew at an average annual rate of 5.7 percent to $10 trillion (current U.S. dollars) between 1990 and 2000.[14] In comparison, Canadian GDP grew by 2.6 percent annually and Mexican GDP grew by 9.1 percent annually (both in current U.S. dollars).

Trade with NAFTA partners has increased in part because Canada and Mexico are important areas for USDIA. Intrafirm trade across national borders often increases when companies invest in branch plants, subsidiaries, or alliances in other countries. Also, direct investment often offers cross-border opportunities for engineering and construction firms, which in turn may rely on home country suppliers.

In 2000, USDIA to Canada and Mexico totaled $162 billion, accounting for 13 percent of total USDIA to all countries (table 7). U.S. investment in Canada is larger than in Mexico, but rapid increases in trade with Mexico are reflected by a faster annual growth rate in Mexican investments. From 1994

---

[14] In inflation-adjusted real (chained 1996) dollars, between 1990 and 2000, U.S. GDP growth averaged 3.3 percent per year reaching $9.3 trillion in 2000.

Table 7
U.S. Direct Investment Abroad (USDIA) in Canada and Mexico
and in Other Selected Regions: 1994–2000
(Millions of dollars)

	1994	1995	1996	1997	1998	1999	2000	Percentage change, 1994–2000	Annual growth rate, 1994–2000
Total, all countries	**612,893**	**699,015**	**795,195**	**871,316**	**1,000,703**	**1,130,789**	**1,244,654**	**103.1**	**12.5**
Canada	74,221	83,498	89,592	96,626	98,200	111,051	126,421	70.3	9.3
Mexico	16,968	16,873	19,351	24,050	26,657	32,262	35,414	108.7	13.0
NAFTA partner totals	91,189	100,371	108,943	120,676	124,857	143,313	161,835	77.5	10.0
NAFTA partner share of total USDIA (percent)	14.9	14.4	13.7	13.8	12.5	12.7	13.0		
Investment in Mexico relative to investment in Canada (percent)	22.9	20.2	21.6	24.9	27.1	29.1	28.0		
Europe	297,133	344,596	389,378	425,139	518,433	588,341	648,731	118.3	13.9
Latin America and other Western Hemisphere countries	116,478	131,377	155,925	180,818	196,755	220,705	239,388	105.5	12.8

NOTE: The Bureau of Economic Analysis defines U.S. direct investment abroad as the ownership or control, directly or indirectly, by 1 U.S. person of 10 percent or more of the voting securities of an incorporated foreign business enterprise or the equivalent interest in an unincorporated foreign business enterprise.

SOURCE: U.S. Department of Commerce, Bureau of Economic Analysis, International Accounts Data, "U.S. Direct Investment Abroad," available at http://www.bea.doc.gov/bea/di/dia-ctry.htm, as of July 25, 2001.

to 2000, USDIA in NAFTA partners grew at a combined average annual rate of 10 percent, slower than the growth rate of total U.S. investments to all countries, which was 12.5 percent. Investments in Canada grew more slowly than those in Mexico over this period. However, the investments in Mexico declined slightly in 1995, the year following the peso crisis, as peso-denominated assets became less valuable relative to U.S. dollars.[15] Investments in Mexico rebounded in 1996 and have increased at a slightly faster rate than U.S. investments in Latin America and Western Hemisphere countries, at 12.8 percent.

Passenger Travel Between the United States and Canada and Mexico

In 1999, approximately 300 million visits (or roundtrips) were recorded between the United States and Mexico and the United States and Canada, an increase of just over 5 percent from the

---

[15] U.S. International Trade Commission, *Examination of U.S. Inbound and Outbound Direct Investment*, Staff Research Study 26, Publication 3383 (Washington, DC: January 2001).

285 million North American resident cross-border visits made in 1990 (box 2). About 80 percent of all travel back and forth across the borders is done on same-day trips, with the remaining 20 percent of trips involving an overnight stay. The vast majority of people travel by personal vehicle, with walking, airplane, and bus the other primary modes of transportation (tables 8 and 9).

Same-Day Travel

Same-day excursions dominate travel between the United States and its two neighbors, accounting for about 87 percent of total travel between the United States and Mexico and about 66 percent of total travel between the United States and Canada (based on 1999 data, the most recent year for which comprehensive figures are available).

Canadians cite pleasure as the most common reason for same-day travel to the United States, accounting for 53 percent in 1999 (table 10). About 7 percent cited business as their main reason to travel, while another 11 percent came to visit friends and relatives. Trip purpose shares for U.S. residents traveling to Canada are very similar. Comparable data on the Mexican border are not available.

Same-day travel between Canada and the United States declined dramatically between 1990 and 1999, dropping from 76 million to 58 million visits. The decline is partly a result of the unfavorable exchange rate for the Canadian dollar (figure 7). All trip purposes were affected, but the decline was most pronounced for pleasure and business trips. Motor vehicle travel shows the greatest drop, while air travel by Canadians increased over this period.

Box 2
International Travel Data

Data in this section are from multiple sources that use different time series. Total international travel data cited here include both same-day and overnight trips, and are derived from travel surveys conducted by Canada and Mexico as well as regulatory data from the U.S. Immigration and Naturalization Service.

Overnight travel data are available for 2000 from the International Trade Administration (ITA), U.S. Department of Commerce. However same-day travel data, and consequently total international travel data, are only available for 1999. Therefore, this report uses data for both years.

The Canadian and Mexican travel survey data, as well as data released by ITA, are based on travel by residents of each country to the other two countries. Therefore, these data do not capture the entry of all persons into the United States along the U.S.-Canadian or U.S.-Mexican borders.

This report also uses border-crossing data from the U.S. Customs Service, which measure the entry of all persons into the United States along the north and south borders, but without the travel and trip characteristics provided by the Canadian and Mexican travel survey data. Border-crossing data indicate a total of 388 million entries in 1999, and count any person entering the United States, including U.S., Canadian, and Mexican residents as well as residents of other countries. Because of this distinction, the travel survey data will not correspond to the border-crossing data. Both data sources are used in this discussion, with travel survey data presented to assess modal choice and trip purposes and border-crossing data to illustrate activity at particular border-crossing infrastructure points.

Table 8
Canada-U.S./U.S.-Canada Travel by Mode of Transportation
(Thousands of roundtrips)

	1990		1996		1999		Percentage change, 1990–1999
	Number	Percent	Number	Percent	Number	Percent	
Canadian resident overnight travel to the United States	**17,262**	**100.0**	**15,301**	**100.0**	**14,116**	**100.0**	**−18.2**
Air	4,039	23.4	4,496	29.4	4,962	35.2	22.9
Land							
Motor vehicles	12,770	74.0	10,251	67.0	8,563	60.7	−32.9
Personal vehicles	12,164	70.5	9,579	62.6	7,869	55.7	−35.3
Intercity and charter buses	606	3.5	672	4.4	694	4.9	14.5
Intercity rail	36	0.2	33	0.2	35	0.2	−2.8
Other[1]	416	2.4	521	3.4	556	3.9	33.7
Canadian resident same-day travel to the United States	**53,171**	**100.0**	**37,398**	**100.0**	**28,081**	**100.0**	**−47.2**
Air	137	0.3	124	0.3	150	0.5	9.5
Land							
Motor vehicles	52,629	99.0	37,159	99.4	27,807	99.0	−47.2
Personal vehicles	51,829	97.5	36,267	97.0	27,107	96.5	−47.7
Intercity and charter buses	800	1.5	892	2.4	700	2.5	−12.5
Intercity rail	N	N	N	N	N	N	N
Other[1]	405	0.8	115	0.3	124	0.4	−69.4
U.S. resident overnight travel to Canada	**12,252**	**100.0**	**12,909**	**100.0**	**15,180**	**100.0**	**23.9**
Air	2,372	19.4	3,047	23.6	3,760	24.8	58.5
Land							
Motor vehicles	9,103	74.3	9,097	70.5	10,419	68.6	14.5
Personal vehicles	8,381	68.4	8,325	64.5	9,609	63.3	14.7
Intercity and charter buses	722	5.9	772	6.0	810	5.3	12.2
Intercity rail	N	N	72	0.6	101	0.7	N
Other[1]	778	6.3	692	5.4	900	5.9	15.7
U.S. resident same-day travel to Canada	**22,482**	**100.0**	**25,563**	**100.0**	**29,450**	**100.0**	**31.0**
Air	165	0.7	365	1.4	525	1.8	218.2
Land							
Motor vehicles	21,412	95.2	24,700	96.6	28,315	96.1	32.2
Personal vehicles	20,692	92.0	23,804	93.1	27,318	92.8	32.0
Intercity and charter buses	720	3.2	896	3.5	997	3.4	38.5
Intercity rail	N	N	6	–	15	N	N
Other[1]	905	4.0	492	1.9	595	2.0	−34.3

[1] Other includes boaters, pedestrians, and cyclists.

KEY: – = value too small to report; N = data are nonexistent.

SOURCE: Statistics Canada, *International Travel: Travel Between Canada and Other Countries (Touriscope)*, Catalogue No. 66-201-XPB (Ottawa, Ontario: Various years).

In contrast to the U.S.-Canadian situation, same-day travel between the United States and Mexico increased markedly, by approximately 19 percent from 1990 to 1999. This trend was balanced between the two countries' residents as same-day travel in both directions increased at comparable rates; the number of

Table 9
Mexico-U.S./U.S.-Mexico Travel by Mode of Transportation
(Thousands of roundtrips)

	1990		1996		1999		Percentage change, 1990–1999
	Number	Percent	Number	Percent	Number	Percent	
Mexican resident overnight travel to the United States	**7,040**	**100.0**	**8,709**	**100.0**	**9,934**	**100.0**	**41.1**
Air	959	13.6	983	11.3	1,281	12.9	33.5
Land	6,081	86.4	7,726	88.7	8,654	87.1	42.3
Mexican resident same-day travel to the United States	**91,494**	**100.0**	**94,399**	**100.0**	**107,031**	**100.0**	**17.0**
Air	N	N	N	N	N	N	N
Land	91,494	100.0	94,399	100.0	107,031	100.0	17.0
U.S. resident overnight travel to Mexico	**16,377**	**100.0**	**20,302**	**100.0**	**17,577**	**100.0**	**7.3**
Air	3,635	22.2	5,361	26.4	5,835	33.2	60.5
Land	12,742	77.8	14,941	73.6	11,742	66.8	−7.8
U.S. resident same-day travel to Mexico	**64,038**	**100.0**	**66,859**	**100.0**	**77,778**	**100.0**	**21.5**
Air	N	N	N	N	N	N	N
Land	64,038	100.0	66,859	100.0	77,778	100.0	21.5

KEY: N = data are nonexistent.

NOTE: Detailed data for land modes are not available.

SOURCE: Banco de México, Dirección General de Investigación Económica, Dirección de Medición Económica, 1999 and 2001.

same-day trips made by Americans to Mexico jumped by 21 percent between 1990 and 1999, while the number of Mexican same-day trips to the United States climbed by 17 percent during this period. The rate of growth for same-day travel between the United States and Mexico was especially rapid toward the close of the decade. Buoyed by strong economic growth in both countries, total same-day trips between the two nations leapt by nearly 13 percent from 1996 to 1999 alone.

Data show that the vast majority of same-day travelers cross the border in personal vehicles, especially along the Mexican border, which accounts for almost three-quarters of the passenger movement across the U.S. border by land. Border-crossing data also show that 290 million people entered the United States from Mexico in 2000 (table 11), approximately 800,000 a day, up from about 750,000 a day in 1998.[16] About 16 percent of

[16] U.S. Customs personnel collect border-crossing/entry data for all U.S. land, air, and maritime ports. These numbers reflect all entries, and it is not possible to divide these data into separate entries for same-day and overnight travel or by country of residence for the traveler. Additionally, please note that, for border-crossing figures, the total number of people is not the number of unique individuals, but rather indicates the number of border crossings. Multiple crossings by the same individual would count as multiple border crossings. Such is not the case for same-day and overnight travel data (collected by other U.S. government, Canadian, and Mexican agencies), which are always referred to as visits or trips.

Table 10
Canada-U.S./U.S.-Canada Travel by Trip Purpose
(Thousands of roundtrips)

	1990		1996		1999		Percentage change, 1990–1999
	Number	Percent	Number	Percent	Number	Percent	
Canadian resident overnight travel to the United States	**17,262**	**100.0**	**15,301**	**100.0**	**14,116**	**100.0**	**−18.2**
Pleasure/tourism	10,586	61.3	8,810	57.6	7,365	52.2	−30.4
Business	1,972	11.4	2,422	15.8	2,685	19.0	36.2
Visit family and friends	2,701	15.6	2,653	17.3	2,755	19.5	2.0
Other[1]	2,003	11.6	1,418	9.3	1,311	9.3	−34.5
Canadian resident same-day travel to the United States	**53,171**	**100.0**	**37,398**	**100.0**	**28,081**	**100.0**	**−47.2**
Pleasure/tourism	34,159	64.2	23,198	62.0	14,879	53.0	−56.4
Business	3,567	6.7	2,899	7.8	1,857	6.6	−47.9
Visit family and friends	4,703	8.8	3,235	8.7	3,125	11.1	−33.6
Other[1]	10,741	20.2	8,066	21.6	8,220	29.3	−23.5
U.S. resident overnight travel to Canada	**12,252**	**100.0**	**12,909**	**100.0**	**15,180**	**100.0**	**23.9**
Pleasure/tourism	7,012	57.2	7,392	57.3	8,709	57.4	24.2
Business	1,729	14.1	1,970	15.3	2,352	15.5	36.0
Visit family and friends	2,602	21.2	2,221	17.2	2,717	17.9	4.4
Other[1]	909	7.4	1,325	10.3	1,402	9.2	54.2
U.S. resident same-day travel to Canada	**22,482**	**100.0**	**25,563**	**100.0**	**29,450**	**100.0**	**31.0**
Pleasure/tourism	10,958	48.7	13,018	50.9	14,163	48.1	29.2
Business	1,967	8.7	1,778	7.0	1,539	5.2	−21.8
Visit family and friends	5,385	24.0	3,895	15.2	4,088	13.9	−24.1
Other[1]	4,172	18.6	6,872	26.9	9,660	32.8	131.5

[1] Other includes personal, in-transit, shopping, educational study, and other trip purposes.

SOURCES: Statistics Canada, *International Travel, Travel Between Canada and Other Countries (Touriscope)*, Catalogue No. 66-201-XPB (Ottawa, Ontario: Various years); and Statistics Canada, special tabulations, 1998.

the people entered the United States from Mexico on foot, while most of the rest came in personal vehicles. Approximately 250,000 personal vehicles cross into the United States everyday from Mexico, with the largest share by far entering El Paso, Texas, and San Ysidro, California (table 12 and see also box 3 on pages 29–31). San Ysidro also handles about 300 buses each day.

Similar border-crossing data show that the number of people

Figure 7
Currency Exchange Rates: 1990–2000

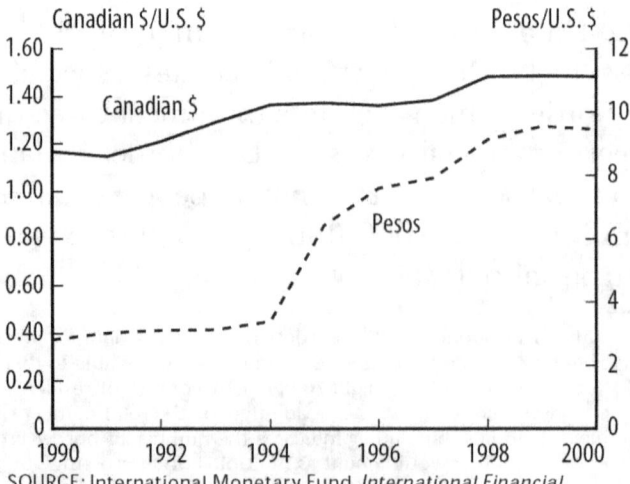

SOURCE: International Monetary Fund, *International Financial Statistics Yearbook 2000* (Washington, DC: 2001).

Table 11
Incoming Passengers by Mode: 1997–2000

	1997		1998		1999		2000	
	Number (thousands)	Percent	Number (thousands)	Percent	Number (thousands)	Percent	Number (thousands)	Percent
From Mexico								
Passengers on trains	U	U	13	–	17	–	18	–
Passengers on buses	U	U	3,639	1.3	3,495	1.2	3,466	1.2
Pedestrians	45,000	17.9	44,477	16.2	48,186	16.4	47,090	16.2
Passengers in personal vehicles	206,113	82.1	226,104	82.4	242,613	82.4	239,795	82.6
Total	**251,112**	**100.0**	**274,232**	**100.0**	**294,311**	**100.0**	**290,368**	**100.0**
From Canada								
Passengers on trains	U	U	241	0.3	187	0.2	270	0.3
Passengers on buses	U	U	3,951	4.3	4,366	4.5	4,873	5.1
Pedestrians	520	U	585	0.6	587	0.6	585	0.6
Passengers in personal vehicles	90,731	U	88,127	94.9	92,470	94.7	90,047	94.0
Total	**U**	**U**	**92,904**	**100.0**	**97,610**	**100.0**	**95,775**	**100.0**

KEY: – = value too small to report; U = data are unavailable.

NOTE: Data for passengers in personal vehicles include the driver. Personal vehicles are automobiles, minivans, sport utility vehicles, and pickups.

SOURCES: U.S. Department of Transportation, Bureau of Transportation Statistics, special tabulation, June 2001; based on U.S. Department of Treasury, U.S. Customs Service, Mission Support Services, Office of Field Operations, *Operations Management Database CD.*

Table 12
Top 10 U.S.-Mexico Border Crossings for Incoming Passengers and Personal Vehicles: 2000

Rank	U.S. Customs port/crossing	Passengers in personal vehicles per day	Personal vehicles per day	Daily port share of personal vehicles crossing U.S.-Mexico border (percent)
1	El Paso, TX	132,658	45,746	18.3
2	San Ysidro, CA	85,001	38,649	15.5
3	Hidalgo, TX	60,131	24,054	9.6
4	Brownsville, TX	53,954	21,582	8.6
5	Laredo, TX	48,980	19,592	7.8
6	Calexico, CA	55,053	18,479	7.4
7	Otay Mesa, CA	29,204	13,275	5.3
8	Nogales, AZ	31,511	12,826	5.1
9	Eagle Pass, TX	23,546	9,199	3.7
10	San Luis, AZ	19,365	7,117	2.8
	Total, top 10 ports	**539,403**	**210,519**	**84.3**
	Total, all U.S.-Mexico border crossings	**656,971**	**249,745**	**100.0**

NOTE: Rank is based on the number of personal vehicle crossings per day.

SOURCES: U.S. Department of Transportation, Bureau of Transportation Statistics, special tabulation, June 2001; based on U.S. Department of Treasury, U.S. Customs Service, Mission Support Services, Office of Field Operations, *Operations Management Database CD.*

coming into the United States from Canada by land is about one-third of the number entering from Mexico, about 96 million in 2000, or 260,000 a day on average.[17] Most of these enter in personal vehicles—about 100,000 a day on the Canadian border. Detroit and Buffalo-Niagara handle the heaviest traffic, half the amount of the most active crossing points on the Mexican border (table 13). The crossing points in the Buffalo-Niagara area also handle about 180 buses each day on average.

Overnight Travel

About half of international overnight travel (travel spanning more than one day) involving the United States is to and from Canada and Mexico. In 2000, a record 51 million international overnight trips were made to the United States, 29 percent from Canada and another 20 percent from Mexico (table 14). U.S. residents made 61 million overnight trips in 2000, with Mexico, their top desti-

---

[17] See box 2 on page 17 for a discussion of data sources.

Table 13
Top 10 U.S.-Canada Border Crossings for Incoming Passengers and Personal Vehicles: 2000

Rank	U.S. Customs port/crossing	Passengers in personal vehicles per day	Personal vehicles per day	Daily port share of personal vehicles crossing U.S.-Canada border (percent)
1	Detroit, MI	59,518	22,905	22.6
2	Buffalo-Niagara, NY	45,269	20,980	20.7
3	Blaine, WA	22,560	9,129	9.0
4	Port Huron, MI	18,810	6,390	6.3
5	Calais, ME	8,525	3,875	3.8
6	Sault Ste. Marie, MI	10,634	3,498	3.5
7	Massena, NY	8,340	2,987	3.0
8	Champlain-Rouses Pt., NY	7,526	2,685	2.7
9	Sumas, WA	5,583	2,243	2.2
10	Derby Line, VT	4,144	2,190	2.2
	Total, top 10 ports	**190,909**	**76,883**	**76.0**
	Total, all U.S.-Canada border crossings	**246,704**	**101,137**	**100.0**

NOTE: Rank is based on the number of personal vehicle crossings per day.

SOURCES: U.S. Department of Transportation, Bureau of Transportation Statistics, special tabulation, June 2001; based on U.S. Department of Treasury, U.S. Customs Service, Mission Support Services, Office of Field Operations, *Operations Management Database CD.*

Table 14
Top 15 Countries for Overnight Travel to the United States: 2000

Rank	Country	Number (thousands)	Percent
1	Canada	14,594	28.7
2	Mexico	10,322	20.3
3	Japan	5,061	9.9
4	United Kingdom	4,703	9.2
5	Germany	1,786	3.5
6	France	1,087	2.1
7	Brazil	737	1.4
8	South Korea	662	1.3
9	Italy	612	1.2
10	Venezuela	577	1.1
11	Netherlands	553	1.1
12	Australia	540	1.1
13	Argentina	534	1.0
14	Taiwan	457	0.9
15	China[1]	453	0.9
	Total, top 15 countries	**42,678**	**83.9**
	Total, all countries	**50,891**	**100.0**

[1] China includes Hong Kong.

NOTE: Overnight travel includes trips of at least one night or longer by residents of each country. Data for Canada and Mexico do not include same-day travel, which accounts for the majority of trips by Canadian and Mexican residents to the United States.

SOURCE: U.S. Department of Commerce, International Trade Administration, Office of Tourism Industries, "Arrivals to the U.S. 2000 & 1999," available at http://tinet.ita.doc.gov, as of July 18, 2001.

Table 15
Top 15 Countries Visited by U.S. Residents for Overnight Travel: 2000

Rank	Country	Number (thousands)	Percent
1	Mexico	18,849	31.0
2	Canada	15,114	24.9
3	United Kingdom	4,189	6.9
4	France	2,927	4.8
5	Germany	2,309	3.8
6	Italy	2,148	3.5
7	China[1]	1,476	2.4
8	Japan	1,262	2.1
8	Spain	1,262	2.1
9	Netherlands	1,101	1.8
10	Switzerland	994	1.6
11	Bahamas	913	1.5
12	Jamaica	886	1.5
13	Republic of Korea	779	1.3
14	Ireland	725	1.2
15	Australia	698	1.1
	Total, top 15 countries	**55,632**	**91.5**
	Total, all countries	**60,816**	**100.0**

[1] China includes Hong Kong.

NOTE: Overnight travel includes trips of at least one night or longer. Data for Canada and Mexico do not include same-day travel, which accounts for the majority of trips by U.S. residents to both of these countries.

SOURCE: U.S. Department of Commerce, International Trade Administration, Office of Tourism Industries, "U.S. Resident Travel Abroad: Historical Visitation—Outbound 1990–2000 (One or More Nights)," available at http://tinet.ita.doc.gov, as of July 18, 2001.

nation, accounting for a third of these trips (table 15). For Americans, Canada was the second most visited overnight destination with 25 percent of total trips.

Overnight travel between the United States and other countries increased 33 percent between 1990 and 2000, from 84 million to 112 million (figures 8 and 9). Reflecting the increasing globalization of the economy and lower airfares, travel between the United States and countries overseas grew much faster than with our North American neighbors, Canada and Mexico. Overnight trips to and from overseas countries increased 71 percent between 1990 and 2000, compared with only 11 percent between the United States and Canada and Mexico.

Figure 8
Overnight Trips to the United States: 1990–2000

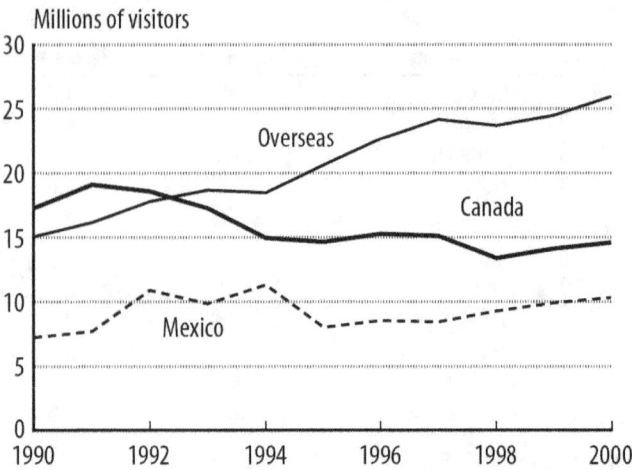

Millions of visitors

NOTE: Overnight travel includes trips of at least one night or longer. Data for Canada and Mexico do not include same-day travel.

SOURCES: U.S. Department of Commerce, International Trade Administration, Office of Tourism Industries, "International Visitors (Inbound) and U.S. Residents (Outbound) (1990–2000)," and "Arrivals to the U.S. 1999 & 1998 (All Countries by Residency), and in Rank Order within Region," available at http://tinet.ita.doc.gov, as of Aug. 3, 2001.

Figure 9
U.S. Resident International Overnight Trips: 1990–2000

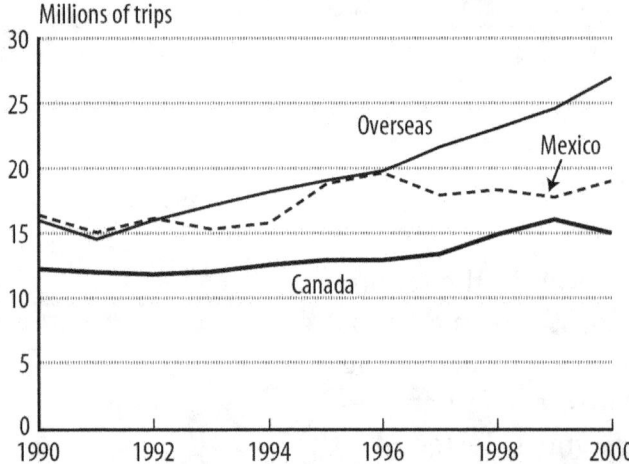

Millions of trips

NOTE: Overnight travel includes trips of at least one night or longer. Data for Canada and Mexico do not include same-day travel.

SOURCES: U.S. Department of Commerce, International Trade Administration, Office of Tourism Industries, "International Visitors (Inbound) and U.S. Residents (Outbound) (1990–2000)," and "Arrivals to the U.S. 1999 & 1998 (All Countries by Residency), and in Rank Order within Region," available at http://tinet.ita.doc.gov, as of Aug. 3, 2001.

In contrast to same-day trips, total overnight traffic between the United States and Canada and between the United States and Mexico is roughly comparable. The direction of overnight travel between the countries is very different, however, resulting, in large measure, from the much wider disparity in income between residents of the United States and Mexico than exists between the United States and Canada. In 2000, Americans took only 1 million more overnight trips to Canada than Canadians did to the United States.[18] However, Americans took nearly 9 million more overnight trips to Mexico than Mexicans took to the United States. This is despite the fact that the population of Canada is about 30 million compared with 100 million Mexicans and 280 million Americans.

As with same-day travel, ground transportation, particularly the use of personal vehicles, is still the primary mode for North American overnight travel. Air, however, is relied on more heavily for overnight trips than it is for same-day trips. Tables 8 and 9 (pages 18 and 19) illustrate air travel's increasing modal share of all international North American trips from 1990 to 1999, with the single exception of Mexican travel to the United States.[19] About 65 percent of overnight trips between

[18] Data for overnight trips by Americans to Canada and Canadians to the United States are from U.S. Department of Commerce, International Trade Administration, Office of Tourism Industries, "U.S. Resident Travel to Canada, Mexico and Overseas Countries, Historical Visitation Outbound: 1990–2000," available at http://tinet.ita.doc.gov, as of August 2001.

[19] Statistics Canada, International Travel, *Travel Between Canada and Other Countries (Touriscope)*, Catalogue No. 66-201-XPB (Ottawa, Ontario: Various years); and Statistics Canada, special tabulations, 1998.

the United States and Canada were made by land modes (the vast majority in personal vehicles) in 1999, down from 74 percent in 1990. In 1999, approximately 74 percent of overnight trips between the United States and Mexico were made by land modes, down from about 80 percent in 1990.

During the 1990s, travel survey data show air travel growing from 22 percent to about 30 percent of overnight trips between the United States and Canada, and from 20 percent to 26 percent for such trips between the United States and Mexico. Carrier data also show the importance of air travel between the North American countries. In 2000, Canada-U.S. passenger traffic accounted for 18.2 million trips, while U.S.-Mexico traffic reached 16.3 million trips.[20] The top three North American air passenger city pairs are Toronto-New York, Toronto-Chicago, and Los Angeles-Mexico City.

Passenger Travel and the Balance of Payments

International passenger travel generates much revenue for transportation carriers, hotels, restaurants, and other travel-related businesses. The United States had a 7 percent share of all international overnight visitors in 2000 and a 17 percent share of worldwide international overnight visitor receipts.[21] Expenditures by international visitors amounted to $82 billion in 2000, nearly $18 billion more than U.S. residents paid on international trips[22] (table 16). Passenger fares paid by international travelers to U.S. transportation providers brought in another $21 billion, but this was $3.4 billion less than what U.S. residents paid to transportation service providers in other countries.[23] Although Canada and Mexico are the most heavily traveled countries for U.S. residents, U.S. residents had the largest total travel and

[20] U.S. Department of Transportation, Bureau of Transportation Statistics, Office of Airline Information, Segment T-100 data track nonstop commercial traffic traveling between international points and U.S. airports. Segment T-100 data include both scheduled and chartered flights (aircraft with 60 seats or more). Therefore, passenger volume in particular markets, such as certain U.S.-Canada markets, is understated.

[21] U.S. Department of Commerce, International Trade Administration, Office of Tourism Industries, personal communication, July 2001.

[22] Travel expenditures include goods and services (e.g., food, lodging, recreation, gifts, entertainment, and local transportation) purchased when visiting a foreign country. A traveler is a person who visits a country for less than one year, except diplomats and military and civilian government personnel. Educational and medical expenditures are not included. Expenditures on same-day trips by Americans, Canadians, and Mexicans are included.

[23] International passenger fares refer to fares paid by residents of one country to airline and vessel operators in another country on trips to or from the two countries involved.

Table 16
Top 6 Countries by U.S. Travel Receipts: 2000
(Millions of dollars)

Country	Receipts from foreign citizens		Payments by U.S. residents		Balance (receipts minus payments)	
	Travel	Passenger fares	Travel	Passenger fares	Travel	Passenger fares
Japan	10,238	3,773	2,872	938	7,366	2,835
United Kingdom	9,957	2,751	6,368	4,746	3,589	−1,995
Canada	7,055	1,713	6,367	827	688	886
Mexico	4,937	1,027	6,646	920	−1,709	107
Germany	4,035	1,090	2,678	1,924	1,357	−834
France	2,637	1,016	3,634	1,183	−997	−167
Total, top 6 countries	**38,859**	**11,370**	**28,565**	**10,538**	**10,294**	**832**
Total, all countries	**82,042**	**20,745**	**64,537**	**24,197**	**17,505**	**−3,452**

NOTES: **Travel**—The travel accounts cover purchases of goods and services by U.S. citizens traveling abroad and by foreign travelers in the United States for business or personal reasons. These goods and services include food, lodging, recreation, gifts, entertainment, and other items incidental to a foreign visit.

Passenger fares—The passenger fare accounts cover fares paid by residents of one country to airline and vessel operators (carriers) of another country.

Receipts consist of fares received by U.S. air carriers from foreign residents for travel between the United States and foreign coun-tries and between two foreign points and for travel on U.S. cruise vessels.

Payments consist of fares paid by U.S. residents to foreign air carriers for travel between the United States and foreign countries and for travel on foreign cruise vessels.

SOURCE: U.S. Department of Commerce, Bureau of Economic Analysis, Survey of Current Business, July 2001, tables 1 and 10.

passenger fare expenditures for visits to the United Kingdom. In 2000, residents of Japan and the United Kingdom spent more than other international travelers to the United States, followed by Canada and Mexico.

Receipts from Canadians traveling to the United States declined by 21 percent (in inflation-adjusted terms) between 1990 and 2000, and receipts from Mexican travelers declined by 24 percent over this period (figures 10 and 11). With growth in the payments to businesses in Canada (42 percent) and Mexico (8 percent) during this time, the travel balance of payments with Canada shrank dramatically and went from positive to negative with Mexico. Passenger fare receipts and payments increased with both Canada and Mexico. However, the U.S. trade balance on passenger fares with Mexico fluctuated to a greater extent between 1990 and 2000. Thus, the U.S. trade balance with both countries for passenger fares improved and then deteriorated over the period, ending in 2000 near to where it began in 1990.

Figure 10
Travel and Passenger Fare Transactions with Canada: 1990–2000

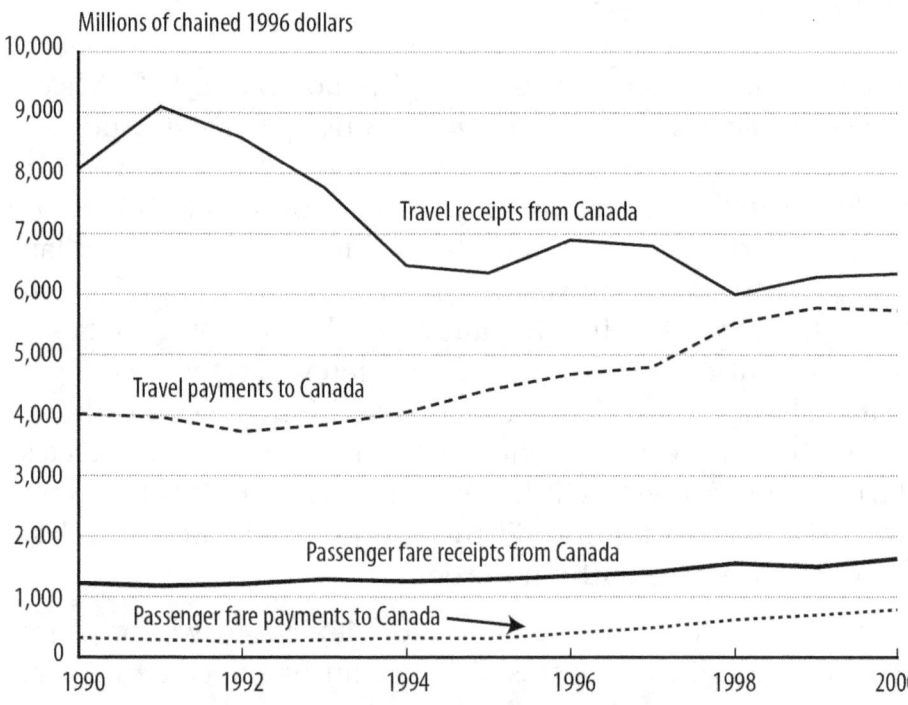

Millions of chained 1996 dollars

Travel receipts from Canada

Travel payments to Canada

Passenger fare receipts from Canada

Passenger fare payments to Canada →

SOURCE: U.S. Department of Commerce, Bureau of Economic Analysis, *Survey of Current Business*, July 2001.

Figure 11
Travel and Passenger Fare Transactions with Mexico: 1990–2000

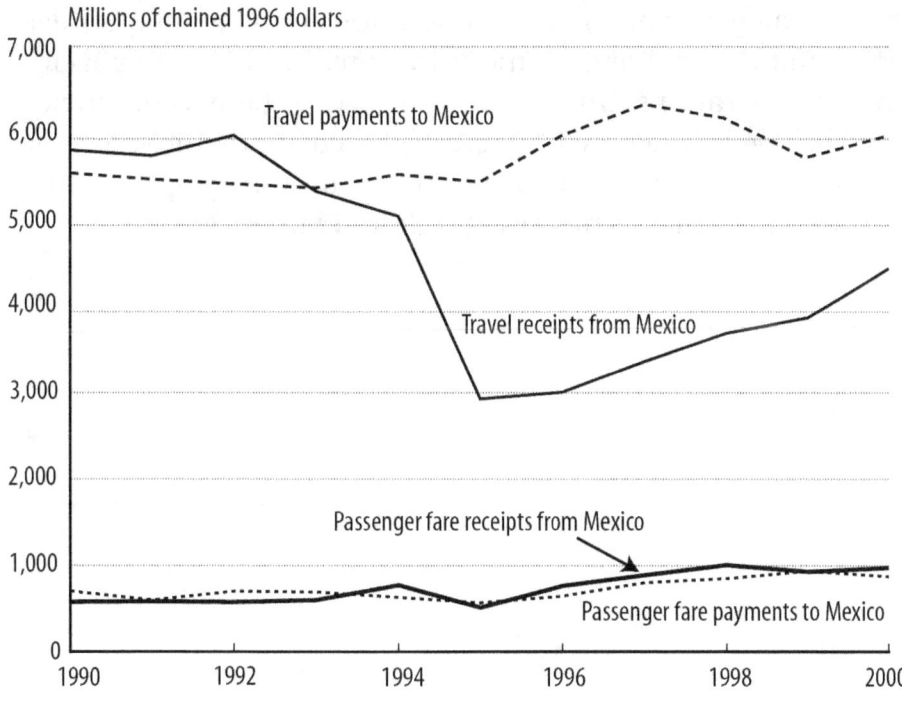

Millions of chained 1996 dollars

Travel payments to Mexico

Travel receipts from Mexico

Passenger fare receipts from Mexico

Passenger fare payments to Mexico

SOURCE: U.S. Department of Commerce, Bureau of Economic Analysis, *Survey of Current Business*, July 2001.

Conclusion: Where Freight and Passengers Meet

The dominant gateways on the U.S.-Canadian and U.S.-Mexican borders serve as both passenger and freight crossing points. The border ports of Detroit, Michigan, and Buffalo, New York, were the busiest land gateways for travel in personal vehicles by Canadians and Americans and also the leading U.S.-Canadian gateways for trade by all surface modes. On the U.S.-Mexican border, the dominant freight gateways, Laredo and El Paso, Texas, were also among the leading gateways for passenger crossings. In addition, the San Ysidro and Otay Mesa, California, crossings were major gateways for personal-use vehicles and trucks, respectively. The busiest city pairs for air travel were New York-Toronto for the northern border and Los Angeles-Mexico City for the southern border.

As U.S. trade with Canada and Mexico grows, pressure on border and gateway infrastructure can be expected to rise, with the potential to increase congestion levels, alter current traffic flow patterns, and create demand for congestion mitigation strategies, particularly at intermodal connectors where multiple modes meet. Technologies such as pre-clearance systems and automated entry systems combined with demand management strategies remain possible solutions for changing border capacity and to complement modifications to physical capacity and border operations. Importantly, the use of these technologies will need to be balanced with increased security requirements at U.S. border ports and transportation facilities, in light of the September 2001 attacks against the United States.

Box 3
Spotlight on Two California Gateways: San Ysidro and Otay Mesa

Two of the busiest U.S. border gateways, the San Ysidro and Otay Mesa ports of entry, processed over 41.5 million northbound passengers in personal vehicles and 8 million northbound pedestrians in 2000 (see table below and map on page 30). The crossing station areas, which serve as the main gateways for San Diego-Tijuana passenger traffic, are not only integral parts of the transborder

infrastructure, but also two huge complexes in and of themselves.[1]

[1] The San Ysidro port of entry is located approximately 15 miles (24 kilometers) south of downtown San Diego and 8 miles (13 kilometers) inland from the Pacific Ocean. Southbound border crossers enter Puerta Mexico when leaving San Ysidro. The Otay Mesa port of entry, opened in 1984, is located just over 6 miles (10 kilometers) to the east of the San Ysidro port of entry and is bordered by Mesa de Otay, Mexico, on the south. The Otay Mesa port is accessed by southbound travel on State Route 905 (SR 905) or by following Otay Mesa Road.

Ports of San Ysidro and Otay Mesa, California, Border-Crossing Data: 1996–2000
(Northbound only)

	1996	1997	1998	1999	2000	Percentage change, 1996–2000
Personal vehicles						
San Ysidro	13,782,593	13,213,420	14,474,686	15,269,561	14,106,704	
Otay Mesa	3,377,407	3,800,936	4,326,786	4,480,026	4,845,348	
Total	**17,160,000**	**17,014,356**	**18,801,472**	**19,749,587**	**18,952,052**	**10.4**
Passengers in personal vehicles						
San Ysidro	34,569,739	29,069,523	31,844,311	33,593,034	31,025,343	
Otay Mesa	8,294,261	8,362,058	9,518,925	9,856,055	10,659,498	
Total	**42,864,000**	**37,431,581**	**41,363,236**	**43,449,089**	**41,684,841**	**−2.8**
Buses						
San Ysidro	92,355	96,208	107,563	108,025	101,244	
Otay Mesa	19,921	18,586	26,978	46,142	47,683	
Total	**112,276**	**114,794**	**134,541**	**154,167**	**148,927**	**32.6**
Bus passengers						
San Ysidro	878,713	873,411	890,614	854,098	783,762	
Otay Mesa	216,287	196,190	235,288	312,342	845,775	
Total	**1,095,000**	**1,069,601**	**1,125,902**	**1,166,440**	**1,629,537**	**48.8**
Pedestrians						
San Ysidro	8,809,794	7,046,923	6,909,382	7,558,174	7,542,450	
Otay Mesa	583,206	621,517	619,158	684,047	648,756	
Total	**9,393,000**	**7,668,440**	**7,528,540**	**8,242,221**	**8,191,206**	**−12.8**

NOTE: Data for passengers in personal vehicles include the driver. Personal vehicles are automobiles, minivans, sport utility vehicles, and pickups.

SOURCES: U.S. Department of Transportation, Bureau of Transportation Statistics, based on data from U.S. Department of Commerce, U.S. Customs Service, Mission Support Services, Office of Field Operations, Operations Management Database CD.

1996 San Ysidro and aggregate figures are based on: U.S. Department of Transportation, Bureau of Transportation Statistics; U.S. Department of Commerce, U.S. Census Bureau; Statistics Canada; Transport Canada; Instituto Mexicano del Transporte; Instituto Nacional de Estadística, Geografía e Informática; and Secretaría de Comunicaciones y Transportes, North American Transportation in Figures: English Edition, BTS00-05 (Washington, DC: Bureau of Transportation Statistics, 2000), table 9-2b.

(Box 3 continued on next page)

(Box 3 continued)

Border-Crossing Facilities Between California and Mexico

At the San Ysidro entry, due to the extremely heavy traffic volume, there are 24 primary inspection booths designated for passenger vehicles and 16 primary inspection booths designated for pedestrians.[2] In order to handle the 24-hour, 7-day a week crossing activity, between 200 and 275 U.S. Customs agents, as well as over 200 U.S. Immigration and Naturalization Service agents, are stationed at the U.S. side of the port. From the north, two freeways[3] and the San Diego light rail line feed the border station, where extensive parking facilities are located. Adjacent factory outlet stores, fast food restaurants, and motels round out the border area.

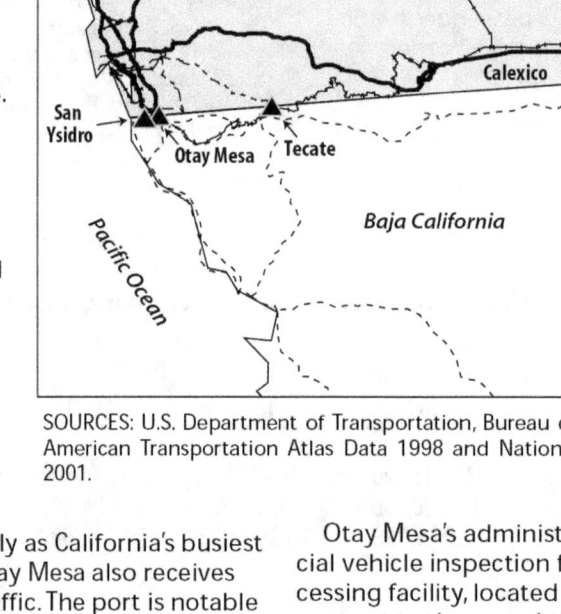

SOURCES: U.S. Department of Transportation, Bureau of Transportation Statistics, North American Transportation Atlas Data 1998 and National Transportation Atlas Database 2001.

Although known principally as California's busiest commercial port of entry, Otay Mesa also receives its fair share of passenger traffic. The port is notable for its proximity to Tijuana International Airport (the airport is situated only a few kilometers west of the border stations).

Otay Mesa's administration maintains a commercial vehicle inspection facility and a passenger processing facility, located one kilometer apart. In contrast to the round-the-clock activity at the San Ysidro port, Otay Mesa only opens its gates to passenger vehicles and pedestrians between the hours of 6:00 am and 10:00 pm (loaded trucks may only gain northbound entry between 8:00 am and 5:00 pm). The limited crossing hours and lighter passenger load at Otay Mesa are reflected in the staff size and lane total at the northbound passenger processing facility—only 45 Customs inspectors and 41 administrative/support employees operate the station's 6 pedestrian booths and 13 primary passenger vehicle inspection lanes. Accordingly, the Otay Mesa crossing area includes fast food restaurants and some retail activity, but is not as well developed for the passenger consumer market as the San Ysidro area. The commercial vehicle inspection facility has 5 primary processing gates and 100 secondary inspection spaces.

Current delays at the San Ysidro gateway have become a regional concern, with the potential for even greater traffic volume in the near future. According to a 2000 survey,[4] San Ysidro's north-

---

[2] In **primary inspections,** passengers and pedestrians state their citizenship, present entry documents when appropriate, and declare goods being carried into the United States. Based on the answers to questions and, for vehicles, a quick visual inspection, individuals and vehicles are allowed to enter. Primary inspection takes between 30 seconds and 2 minutes. Not all commercial vehicles are inspected. Those that are chosen for a primary inspection are assessed visually and their documents reviewed. Primary inspection of commercial vehicles takes between 15 minutes and 3 hours.

Secondary inspections take place in an area apart from the primary inspection station. Vehicles are searched and their occupants questioned. This type of inspection takes from just a few minutes to several hours. Pedestrian secondary inspections include a physical examination of bags and packages.

Commercial vehicles who pass the primary inspection are subject to random selection for a reinspection. Secondary inspection is the same as the primary inspection, but is conducted by privately contracted inspectors who check the reliability and efficiency of the initial inspection.

[3] These are Interstate (I) I-5 and I-805. Both are eight-lane freeways, with I-805 terminating one-half mile from San Ysidro and connecting/merging with I-5.

[4] Parsons Transportation Group, *Final Report: San Diego-Baja California Cross-Border Transportation Study* (San Diego, CA: November 2000), p. 24.

bound queue waiting time for passenger vehicles averaged 23.1 minutes during morning peak hours and 25.9 minutes during evening peak hours. The San Ysidro port's infrastructure currently meets traffic demand and the station's authorities can increase capacity by keeping all 24 northbound lanes open longer than the normal 2 hours of full operations. However, a large increase in traffic flow—which is certainly possible over time—could test the port's infrastructure.

Partly to stem future delays, a mostly automated inspection process involving a dedicated commuter lane and electronic inspection technology has been implemented. The technology, called Secure Electronic Network for Travelers' Rapid Inspection (SENTRI) was first installed at Otay Mesa in November 1995. SENTRI allows pre-registered travelers who frequently cross the border to use a special lane offering brief, mostly automated inspections. Two SENTRI lanes opened at San Ysidro in September 2000. For an annual fee of $129,

commuters receive a special radio device that is attached to their vehicle and access to the swiftly moving SENTRI lanes. As vehicles approach the border in the SENTRI lanes, they are screened by the system. An inspector uses a computer to compare digitized photographs and passenger identification numbers with the people in the vehicle. Though little data on San Ysidro's SENTRI system are available, Otay Mesa participants reportedly seldom experience waits of more than three minutes, even at peak hours.

Over the next 20 years, there may be a rise in the number of cross-border trips at these two entry points, especially if strong economic growth continues in Mexico. Regionally, projections show San Diego and northwestern Baja California undergoing growth in population, trade flows, cross-border worker commuting, and jobs. All of these factors may serve to boost traffic flow totals for San Ysidro and Otay Mesa to all-time high levels.

www.ingramcontent.com/pod-product-compliance
Lightning Source LLC
Chambersburg PA
CBHW081623220526

45468CB00010B/3007